Benjamin Netanyahu

Benjamin "Bibi" Netanyahu, born on October 21, 1949, is a prominent Israeli politician who has had a significant impact on the country's political landscape. He has served as the Prime Minister of Israel for multiple terms, making history as the longest-tenured prime minister, with a total of over 16 years in office. Netanyahu is also notable for being the first prime minister born in Israel after its establishment.

Raised in Tel Aviv and Jerusalem by secular Jewish parents, Netanyahu later spent time in the United States, particularly in Philadelphia. In 1967, he returned to Israel to join the Israel Defense Forces, where he became a team leader in the Sayeret Matkal special forces. Netanyahu earned the rank of captain before being honorably discharged. After completing his studies at the Massachusetts Institute of Technology, he worked as an economic consultant for the Boston Consulting Group.

In 1978, Netanyahu returned to Israel and founded the Yonatan Netanyahu Anti-Terror Institute. His career took an international turn when he served as the Permanent Representative of Israel to the United Nations from 1984 to 1988. He gained prominence as the Chairman of the Likud party in 1993, subsequently becoming the Leader of the Opposition.

In 1996, Netanyahu secured a historic victory, defeating Shimon Peres in the election and becoming the first Israeli prime minister elected directly by popular vote. However, his tenure was not without challenges, and he chose to retire from politics after the defeat in the 1999 election. Netanyahu later returned to public service, holding positions such as Minister of Foreign Affairs and Minister of Finance under Ariel Sharon.

The twists and turns of Netanyahu's political career continued when he resumed leadership of Likud in 2005. Following the resignation of Ariel Sharon, he led the opposition from 2006 to 2009 before forming a coalition government and serving as prime minister once again. Netanyahu led Likud to victory in the 2013 and 2015 elections, but subsequent elections in 2019 and 2020 led to a political deadlock.

In his penultimate government, Netanyahu faced the challenges of the COVID-19 pandemic and the 2021 Israel–Palestine crisis. Despite these challenges, his government collapsed in December 2020, leading to a new election in March 2021. Netanyahu returned to the opposition before once again becoming prime minister after the 2022 election.

During his political career, Netanyahu cultivated a close relationship with Donald Trump, leveraging this connection to advance Israel's interests. Trump's presidency saw significant policy shifts, including the recognition of Jerusalem as Israel's capital and the normalization agreements between Israel and various Arab states known as the Abraham Accords.

However, Netanyahu has faced international criticism for his policies on Israeli settlements in the occupied West Bank, considered illegal under international law. In 2019, he was indicted on charges of breach of trust, bribery, and fraud, resulting in his relinquishment of other ministry posts while maintaining the position of prime minister.

Recent events, such as the 2023 Israel–Hamas war triggered by an attack from Hamas, have brought new challenges for Netanyahu's leadership. The criticism he faced for what some have called Israel's biggest intelligence failure in 50 years adds another layer to his complex political legacy.

Early Life and Military Career: A Journey of Leadership and Sacrifice

Born in Tel Aviv in 1949, Benjamin "Bibi" Netanyahu's early years were marked by a rich tapestry of heritage and intellectual influence. His mother, Tzila Segal, hailed from the Ottoman Empire's Mutasarrifate of Jerusalem, while his father, Warsaw-born historian Benzion Netanyahu, played a pivotal role in shaping his understanding of the Jewish Golden age of Spain. The family's commitment to Zionism was evident in Netanyahu's paternal grandfather, Rabbi Nathan Mileikowsky.

As the second of three children, Netanyahu's upbringing initially unfolded in Jerusalem, where he attended Henrietta Szold Elementary School. An evaluation from his 6th-grade teacher highlighted Netanyahu's virtues—courtesy, responsibility, and punctuality. The family later lived in Cheltenham Township, Pennsylvania, from 1956 to 1958 and again from 1963 to 1967, providing the young Netanyahu with a unique perspective on life in the United States.

In Pennsylvania, Netanyahu attended Cheltenham High School, actively participating in the debate club, chess club, and soccer. Dissatisfied with what he perceived as a superficial way of life, he and his brother Yonatan found themselves at odds with the prevailing counterculture movement and liberal sensibilities of the Reform synagogue they attended.

In 1967, Netanyahu returned to Israel after graduating from high school, enlisting in the Israel Defense Forces (IDF). His dedication to service led him to join the elite special forces unit, Sayeret Matkal, where he underwent rigorous combat training. Netanyahu's military service, spanning five years, included participation in cross-border raids during the War of Attrition. Notably, he played a crucial role in the March 1968 Battle of Karameh, an attempt to capture PLO leader Yasser Arafat that ultimately ended in heavy casualties for the IDF.

Throughout his service, Netanyahu rose to the position of team leader, displaying courage and resilience. Wounded multiple times in combat, he participated in missions such as the 1968 Israeli raid on Lebanon and the daring rescue of Sabena Flight 571 in May 1972, where he was shot in the shoulder. After being discharged in 1972, Netanyahu, driven by a sense of duty, returned to Israel in October 1973 to serve in the Yom Kippur War. His contributions included special forces raids along the Suez Canal and a classified commando attack deep inside Syrian territory, showcasing his commitment to the defense of his homeland.

Reflecting on his time with Sayeret Matkal, Netanyahu emphasized the unit's significant impact on his understanding of operational risks and the sacrifices made by soldiers. His military experiences became an indelible part of his character, influencing his future leadership roles in Israeli politics.

Following his military service, Benjamin Netanyahu embarked on an academic journey that took him to the prestigious Massachusetts Institute of Technology (MIT) in the United States. In late 1972, he began his studies in architecture, demonstrating a multidimensional approach to his intellectual pursuits.

Despite briefly returning to Israel to participate in the Yom Kippur War, Netanyahu returned to the United States under the pseudonym Ben Nitay. He exhibited exceptional determination by completing a bachelor's degree in architecture in February 1975. Notably, he achieved this milestone at a swift pace, given the standard four-year duration for such a program. His academic prowess extended further when he earned a master's degree from the MIT Sloan School of Management in June 1976.

Simultaneously, Netanyahu delved into political science, pursuing a doctorate until a profound personal tragedy interrupted his studies. In 1976, his older brother, Yonatan Netanyahu, the commander of the Sayeret Matkal unit that Benjamin had once served in, lost his life during Operation Thunderbolt. This counter-terrorism mission successfully rescued over 100 hostages, predominantly Israelis, who had been hijacked and taken to Entebbe Airport in Uganda. Yonatan's sacrifice marked a poignant moment in Netanyahu's life, forever influencing his perspective and commitment to his country.

At MIT, Netanyahu exhibited extraordinary diligence, undertaking a double-load of coursework while also enrolling in classes at Harvard University. His efficiency was evident in the accelerated completion of his master's degree in just two and a half years. Professor Leon B. Groisser at MIT praised Netanyahu's intellect, organization, and determination, stating, "He did superbly. He was very bright. Organized. Strong. Powerful. He knew what he wanted to do and how to get it done."

During this time, Netanyahu adopted the name Benjamin "Ben" Nitai, a choice made to facilitate pronunciation for Americans. This decision later became a subject of political scrutiny, with rivals questioning his Israeli national identity and loyalty.

In 1976, Netanyahu graduated near the top of his class at the MIT Sloan School of Management, marking the culmination of his academic endeavors. His educational journey, characterized by dedication and the enduring impact of personal loss, laid the foundation for the multifaceted leader he would become in both academia and politics.

From Economic Consultancy to International Diplomacy

After completing his academic pursuits, Netanyahu transitioned into the corporate world, making his mark as an economic consultant for the Boston Consulting Group in Boston, Massachusetts. From 1976 to 1978, he collaborated with notable figures, including Mitt Romney, and formed a lasting friendship. Romney, describing Netanyahu as possessing "a strong personality with a distinct point of view," emphasized their shared experiences and similar perspectives, attributing their "easy communication" to the intellectual rigor of B.C.G.'s training.

In 1978, Netanyahu, still using the name "Ben Nitai," entered the public discourse, appearing on Boston local television to articulate his views on the Israeli-Arab conflict. He underscored the Arab refusal to accept the State of Israel and challenged the prevailing narrative by pointing out the opportunities for a Palestinian state in the West Bank and Gaza Strip during the preceding two decades.

Returning to Israel in the same year, Netanyahu embarked on a diverse career path. From 1978 to 1980, he led the Jonathan Netanyahu Anti-Terror Institute, a non-governmental organization dedicated to the study of terrorism. The institute hosted international conferences that fostered discussions on global terrorism. Transitioning into the corporate sphere, Netanyahu served as the Director of Marketing for Rim Industries in Jerusalem from 1980 to 1982.

His introduction to the political landscape unfolded through connections with Israeli politicians, including Minister Moshe Arens. Appointed as Arens' Deputy Chief of Mission at the Israeli Embassy in Washington, D.C., Netanyahu assumed the role during Arens' ambassadorship to the United States from 1982 to 1984. During the 1982 Lebanon War, Netanyahu, a reservist in Sayeret Matkal, sought release from duty to serve as a spokesperson for Israel in the face of international criticism. He effectively presented Israel's case to the media, establishing an efficient public relations system at the Israeli embassy.

Between 1984 and 1988, Netanyahu expanded his diplomatic experience as the Israeli ambassador to the United Nations. Throughout this period, he cultivated a relationship with Rabbi Menachem M. Schneerson, whom he regarded as "the most influential man of our time." Additionally, Netanyahu formed a friendship with Fred Trump, the father of future U.S. President Donald Trump.

Netanyahu's early career showcased a dynamic blend of corporate expertise, diplomatic acumen, and a commitment to shaping public discourse on the international stage. These experiences laid the groundwork for his future leadership roles in Israeli politics.

Rise to Political Prominence

Returning to Israel in anticipation of the 1988 legislative election, Benjamin Netanyahu aligned himself with the Likud party. In the internal party elections, he secured the fifth position on the Likud's list and went on to be elected as a Knesset member of the 12th Knesset. Initially serving as a deputy to Foreign Minister Moshe Arens and later to David Levy, Netanyahu's relations with Levy soured, leading to an escalating rivalry between the two.

Netanyahu's fluency in English and his role as the principal spokesperson during the Gulf War in 1991 catapulted him onto the international stage. He represented Israel in media interviews, showcasing his articulate communication skills. Subsequently, after the Madrid Conference in 1991, Netanyahu was appointed Deputy Minister in the Israeli Prime Minister's Office.

The Likud party underwent a leadership change in 1993, with Netanyahu emerging victorious in the party leadership election. He secured the position by defeating prominent figures such as Benny Begin and David Levy. With the defeat of the Likud party in the 1992 legislative elections, Netanyahu's ascent to the party leadership marked a significant turning point.

The political landscape shifted following the assassination of Prime Minister Yitzhak Rabin. Shimon Peres, his temporary successor, called for early elections to secure a mandate for advancing the peace process. Netanyahu became the Likud's candidate for prime minister in the 1996 Israeli legislative election, which was historic as the first in which Israelis directly elected their prime minister. Utilizing American Republican political operative Arthur Finkelstein to run his campaign, Netanyahu employed an assertive style that attracted criticism.

Despite being the underdog against the pre-election favorite, Shimon Peres, Netanyahu secured a surprising victory in the 1996 election, making history as the youngest person to hold the position of prime minister and the first to be born in the State of Israel. The wave of suicide bombings shortly before the election played a pivotal role in Peres's downfall, with Netanyahu emphasizing the need for the Palestinian National Authority to fulfill its anti-terrorism obligations. Although Peres's party won more seats in the Knesset elections, Netanyahu formed a government by relying on a coalition with ultra-Orthodox parties, Shas and UTJ. This coalition marked the beginning of Netanyahu's tenure as prime minister, setting the stage for his impactful political career.

Following his defeat by Ehud Barak in the 1999 Israeli prime ministerial election, Benjamin Netanyahu took a temporary hiatus from politics. During this period, he served as a senior consultant with BATM Advanced Communications, an Israeli communications equipment manufacturer, for two years.

The political landscape changed with the fall of the Barak government in late 2000, prompting Netanyahu to express his desire to return to politics. While Barak's resignation was initially intended to lead to elections for the prime minister position only, Netanyahu advocated for general elections to ensure a stable government. Ultimately, he chose not to run for the prime minister position, paving the way for Ariel Sharon's unexpected rise to power in 2001. In 2002, after the Israeli Labor Party left the coalition, creating a vacancy for the position of foreign minister, Prime Minister Ariel Sharon appointed Netanyahu to the role.

Despite his ministerial position, Netanyahu sought to challenge Sharon for the leadership of the Likud party in the 2002 Likud leadership election. However, he was unsuccessful in ousting Sharon from leadership.

On 9 September 2002, a planned speech by Netanyahu at Concordia University in Montreal was canceled due to hundreds of pro-Palestinian protesters overwhelming security and breaking through a glass window. Netanyahu, who was not present at the protest, accused the activists of supporting terrorism and condemned their "mad zealotry." In October 2002, around 200 protesters confronted Netanyahu outside his appearance at Heinz Hall in Pittsburgh, leading to increased security measures for his subsequent speeches in the area.

On 12 September 2002, Netanyahu testified before the U.S. House of Representatives Committee on Oversight and Government Reform about the nuclear threat posed by the Iraqi regime. In his testimony, he expressed certainty that Saddam Hussein was actively working toward developing nuclear weapons and emphasized the potential positive impact of removing Saddam from power on the region.

Following the 2003 Israeli legislative election, Prime Minister Ariel Sharon surprised many observers by offering the position of Foreign Minister to Silvan Shalom and appointing Benjamin Netanyahu as the Finance Minister. Some speculated that Sharon saw Netanyahu as a political threat due to his effectiveness as Foreign Minister and strategically placed him in the Finance Ministry during a time of economic uncertainty to potentially diminish his popularity. Netanyahu accepted the appointment, and the two leaders reached an agreement where Netanyahu would have autonomy as Finance Minister in exchange for his silence on Sharon's management of military and foreign affairs.

As Finance Minister, Netanyahu implemented an economic plan aimed at revitalizing Israel's economy, which had been adversely affected by the Second Intifada. Netanyahu attributed the economic challenges to a bloated public sector and excessive regulations. His plan included a shift toward more liberalized markets, with measures such as reducing the size of the public sector, freezing government spending for three years, and capping the budget deficit at 1%. He introduced a program to reduce welfare dependency, streamlined the taxation system, and cut taxes, significantly lowering the top individual tax rate and the corporate tax rate. Netanyahu also privatized several state assets, including banks, oil refineries, the national airline El Al, and Zim Integrated Shipping Services. Other reforms involved raising retirement ages, liberalizing currency exchange laws, and tackling monopolies and cartels to promote competition.

Netanyahu's economic policies faced opposition from some in the Labor party and within his own Likud party, who viewed them as "Thatcherite" attacks on Israel's social safety net. Despite the criticism, unemployment decreased, economic growth surged, the debt-to-GDP ratio dropped significantly, and foreign investment reached record highs. Netanyahu's tenure as Finance Minister was widely credited with achieving an "economic miracle."

In 2004, Netanyahu threatened to resign unless the Gaza pullout plan was put to a referendum. Although he modified the ultimatum and voted for the program in the Knesset, he later submitted his resignation letter on 7 August 2005, just before the Israeli cabinet voted to approve the initial phase of the withdrawal from Gaza.

During his second term, Netanyahu faced various challenges and engaged in crucial diplomatic and security efforts. In 2009, the U.S. Secretary of State Hillary Clinton expressed support for a Palestinian state, a stance not aligned with Netanyahu's views. He insisted on Palestinian recognition of Israel as a Jewish state for further negotiations. Responding to President Obama's Cairo speech, Netanyahu endorsed a "Demilitarized Palestinian State" while emphasizing Jerusalem's unified status as Israel's capital.

In September 2009, Netanyahu delivered a powerful speech at the United Nations, emphasizing the threat of a nuclear-armed Iran and condemning Iranian President Ahmadinejad's Holocaust denial. Despite international pressure, he announced a partial settlement freeze in November 2009, a move criticized by Palestinians as insufficient. The freeze ended in 2010, leading to renewed construction in the West Bank.

Netanyahu faced criticism for approving new construction in East Jerusalem during a visit by U.S. Vice President Joe Biden in 2010. The subsequent strain in U.S.-Israel relations highlighted ongoing tensions over settlement policies. In September 2010, Netanyahu entered direct talks with the Palestinians, mediated by the Obama administration. However, the 10-month settlement freeze ended, and new construction was approved, causing diplomatic challenges.

In 2011, social justice protests erupted in Israel, focusing on high living costs. Netanyahu responded by appointing the Trajtenberg Committee to address these concerns. Despite promises to implement reforms, gradual adoption occurred due to coalition differences.

Netanyahu's government also approved a plan to establish a nationwide fiber-optic cable network for high-speed internet access. In 2012, he recognized, for the first time, the right of Palestinians to have their own state, although he insisted on its demilitarization. Later that year, Netanyahu's Likud party merged with Avigdor Lieberman's Yisrael Beiteinu, forming a single ballot for the 2013 general elections.

In his fourth term as Israel's Prime Minister, Benjamin Netanyahu navigated through a series of significant events and political challenges, showcasing his leadership on both domestic and international fronts. Following the 2015 election, where Netanyahu's Likud emerged as the leading party with 30 mandates, he skillfully formed a coalition government, including the Jewish Home, United Torah Judaism, Kulanu, and Shas, securing a stable political foundation.

Determined to extend his influence, Netanyahu announced his intention to run for an unprecedented fifth term in the next general election, demonstrating his commitment to shaping the future of Israel. In August 2015, his government tackled economic issues, implementing a two-year budget aimed at agricultural reforms, lowering import duties to alleviate food prices, and initiating changes in the financial sector to enhance competition and reduce fees.

Netanyahu faced controversy in October 2015 when he made provocative claims linking the Grand Mufti of Jerusalem to Adolf Hitler, suggesting a role in the Holocaust. This assertion drew widespread criticism, prompting Netanyahu to clarify that his intent was not to absolve Hitler but to highlight historical complexities surrounding the Palestinian leader at the time.

In March 2016, the coalition encountered a potential crisis as ultra-Orthodox members opposed steps toward non-Orthodox prayer space at the Western Wall, revealing internal tensions. Furthermore, the United States' abstention from UN Security Council Resolution 2334 in December 2016 fueled diplomatic disputes, with Netanyahu strongly criticizing the resolution and U.S. Secretary of State John Kerry's subsequent speech.

Netanyahu's diplomatic engagements remained noteworthy, including his historic visit to Australia in February 2017, marking the first visit by a serving Israeli prime minister. The three-day visit strengthened ties, with Netanyahu and Australian Prime Minister Malcolm Turnbull signing several bilateral agreements, commemorating a century of relations.

In October 2017, following the United States, Netanyahu's government decided to withdraw from UNESCO, citing perceived anti-Israel actions. This decision, officially ratified in December 2017, underscored Israel's stance on international platforms.

Continuing his assertive approach, Netanyahu accused Iran of violating the Iran nuclear deal in April 2018, presenting a cache of documents to support his claims. His stance garnered mixed reactions, with Iran denouncing it as propaganda. Notably, he commended the 2018 North Korea–United States summit, emphasizing its significance in nuclear disarmament efforts.

The Knesset's passing of the Nation-State Bill in July 2018, supported by Netanyahu's coalition government, marked a legislative milestone, viewed by analysts as a right-wing agenda advancement. In the lead-up to the April 2019 Israeli legislative election, Netanyahu played a key role in brokering a deal to unite parties, ensuring they surpassed the electoral threshold.

Throughout this period, Netanyahu's leadership style and strategic maneuvers continued to shape Israel's political landscape, positioning him as a prominent figure on the global stage.

In January 2017, Benjamin Netanyahu found himself under scrutiny as Israeli police initiated investigations into two interconnected cases known as "Case 1000" and "Case 2000." These investigations involved allegations of impropriety and deals made for personal gain. In Case 1000, Netanyahu faced suspicions of receiving inappropriate favors from individuals, including businessman James Packer and Hollywood producer Arnon Milchan. The subsequent Case 2000 focused on purported efforts to strike a deal with Arnon Mozes, the publisher of Yedioth Ahronot, to advance legislation that would weaken Yedioth's competitor, Israel Hayom, in exchange for favorable media coverage.

The gravity of the situation became apparent on August 3, 2017, when Israeli police confirmed that Netanyahu was now a suspect in cases "1000" and "2000," facing allegations involving fraud, breach of trust, and bribery. The stakes rose further when Ari Harow, Netanyahu's former chief of staff, signed an agreement to cooperate with prosecutors, agreeing to testify against the Prime Minister in these cases.

On February 13, 2018, Israeli police recommended corruption charges against Netanyahu, asserting that there was sufficient evidence for charges of bribery, fraud, and breach of trust in both cases. Netanyahu vehemently denied the accusations, labeling them as baseless and affirming his intention to continue serving as prime minister. Economic Crimes Division Director Liat Ben-Ari recommended indictment for both cases on November 25, 2018.

The legal saga intensified on February 28, 2019, when the Israeli attorney general declared his intent to file indictments against Netanyahu on charges of bribery and fraud in three separate cases. Netanyahu faced formal indictment on November 21, 2019, marking a historic moment as the first sitting prime minister in Israel charged with a crime. In adherence to a legal precedent set by the Israeli Supreme Court in 1993, Netanyahu announced on November 23, 2019, that he would relinquish certain ministerial portfolios, pending the resolution of the legal proceedings. The untested issue of whether a sitting prime minister could be compelled to resign due to an indictment lingered.

Netanyahu's official charging followed on January 28, 2020, setting the stage for a landmark criminal trial. Initially slated for March 2020, the trial faced delays due to the global COVID-19 pandemic, eventually commencing on May 24, 2020. As of April 2023, the legal proceedings against Netanyahu continue, marking a critical chapter in the political history of Israel.

the conclusion of his second premiership, Netanyahu assumed the role of the leader of the opposition, marking his third tenure in this position. Despite the transition, Likud retained its status as the largest party in the twenty-fourth Knesset under his leadership. Netanyahu subsequently guided the opposition throughout the course of the 2022 Israeli legislative election.

Netanyahu's sixth term as Prime Minister began on December 29, 2022. During the initial months of this term:

Reforms in the Judicial Branch: Netanyahu's focus on judicial reforms faced widespread criticism. Critics expressed concerns about its negative impact on:

Separation of powers
Office of the Attorney General
Economy
Public health
Women and minorities
Workers' rights
Scientific research
Overall strength of Israel's democracy
Foreign relations
Protests and Defense Minister's Opposition: Public protests, joined by military reservists, intensified. Defense Minister Yoav Gallant opposed the reforms on March 25, citing security concerns. Following his removal, mass protests ensued, leading Netanyahu to agree to a one-month delay until the next Knesset session after Passover.

Settlement Approvals and Repeals: Netanyahu's government approved the legalization of nine settler outposts in the West Bank. Finance Minister Bezalel Smotrich gained significant authority in the West Bank's Civil Administration, drawing condemnation for de facto annexation. Additionally:

A 2005 law dismantling four Israeli settlements was repealed in March 2023.
The procedure for approving settlement construction was shortened, granting authority to the Finance Minister in June 2023.

Construction Boom in Settlements: In the first six months, construction of 13,000 housing units in settlements occurred, almost triple the amount advanced in the entire year of 2022.

Refusal to Send Lethal Weapons to Ukraine: Israel refused to send lethal weapons to Ukraine due to concerns about potential misuse.

War Against Hamas: On October 7, 2023, following a major surprise attack by Palestinian militants from Gaza, Netanyahu declared a state of war against Hamas. He threatened severe actions against Hamas, including turning their hideouts into ruins. The conflict led to increased public dissatisfaction, calls for Netanyahu's resignation, and strained relations with the international community.

Stand on Cease-Fire: On November 11, 2023, Netanyahu rejected calls for a cease-fire, stating that Israel would stand firm against the world if necessary. He emphasized the Israel Defense Forces' continued presence in Gaza and opposition to the return of the Palestinian Authority.

Criticism During Hostage Meeting: On December 5, 2023, Netanyahu faced criticism during a meeting with released Israeli hostages.

Benjamin Netanyahu has been a prominent figure in the Israeli-Palestinian conflict. He opposed the Oslo Accords from their inception, dedicating a chapter in his book to argue against the Oslo Peace Process. Netanyahu, during his term as prime minister in the late 1990s, consistently reneged on commitments made by previous Israeli governments as part of the Oslo peace process. His stance has been a subject of controversy, and he has advocated for an "economic peace" approach based on economic cooperation and joint effort. Netanyahu has also been critical of U.S.-backed peace talks and has emphasized the importance of security arrangements and recognition of Israel as a national state. He played a role in the U.S.-brokered Abraham Accords, which led to the normalization of relations between Israel and Arab countries, including the United Arab Emirates and Bahrain.

Bar-Ilan Speech and Shift in Position

On 14 June 2009, Benjamin Netanyahu delivered a landmark address at Bar-Ilan University, commonly referred to as the "Bar-Ilan speech." This event marked a significant turning point in Netanyahu's approach to the Israeli-Palestinian conflict. The speech, broadcast live in Israel and parts of the Arab world, showcased a departure from his previous stance, as he endorsed the concept of a Palestinian state existing alongside Israel.

In a response to U.S. President Barack Obama's earlier speech in Cairo, Netanyahu outlined his vision for a two-state solution. He called for the establishment of a Palestinian state with a crucial condition – full demilitarization. This meant no standing army, rockets, missiles, or control over its airspace. Netanyahu emphasized that Jerusalem should remain undivided Israeli territory and insisted on Palestinian recognition of Israel as the national state of the Jewish people. Rejecting the right of return for Palestinian refugees, he argued that resettling them within Israel would undermine the country's existence.

While acknowledging the necessity of limiting settlement expansion in the West Bank as outlined in the 2003 Road Map peace proposal, Netanyahu stated that a complete halt was not feasible. He proposed that settlement expansions be restricted based on the "natural growth" of the population, including immigration.

Netanyahu's Bar-Ilan speech generated mixed reactions globally. The Palestinian National Authority rejected the conditions set for a Palestinian state, and Hamas criticized it as reflecting a "racist and extremist ideology." Some leaders advocated for a third intifada, and the Arab League dismissed the address, refusing to recognize Israel as a Jewish state.

Within Netanyahu's governing coalition, right-wing members criticized him for going against the Likud platform by endorsing the creation of a Palestinian state. Opposition party Kadima leader Tzipi Livni questioned the sincerity of Netanyahu's commitment to the two-state solution, suggesting it was a response to international pressure.

On the international stage, various leaders responded differently. The Czech Republic praised Netanyahu's speech, viewing it as a step in the right direction, while President Barack Obama deemed it an "important step forward." However, critics, including former Iranian President Mahmoud Ahmadinejad, referred to it as "bad news."

Netanyahu's Bar-Ilan speech demonstrated a notable shift in his government's position on the peace process, marking a departure from previous reluctance to openly endorse a two-state solution.

Benjamin Netanyahu is recognized as a staunch advocate of free-market principles and has played a pivotal role in shaping Israel's economic landscape. Described as "the advocate of the free-market," Netanyahu, during his first term as prime minister and subsequently as Minister of Finance (2003–2005), implemented substantial reforms that aimed at fostering economic growth, individual initiative, and competition.

In his initial term as prime minister, Netanyahu initiated significant reforms in the banking sector. Barriers to investment abroad were dismantled, mandatory purchases of government securities were eliminated, and direct credit was streamlined. However, his most impactful economic contributions came during his tenure as Minister of Finance.

During his time as Finance Minister, Netanyahu orchestrated a comprehensive overhaul of the Israeli economy. Key initiatives included the introduction of a welfare-to-work program, privatization efforts, downsizing the public sector, and comprehensive tax reforms. His commitment to breaking down monopolies and cartels aimed at promoting healthy competition within the market.

One of the notable tax reforms introduced by Netanyahu was the extension of capital gains taxes from companies to individuals. This move not only broadened the tax base but also led to a reduction in income taxes. The impact of these reforms was significant, with the Israeli economy experiencing a period of robust growth and a substantial decline in unemployment. Commentators widely credited Netanyahu for engineering an "economic miracle" by the end of his tenure.

However, critics have characterized Netanyahu's economic views as influenced by Margaret Thatcher's "popular capitalism." Despite the economic success during his tenure, there has been debate over the implications of these policies on income inequality and social welfare.

Netanyahu defines capitalism as a system that encourages individual initiative and competition for producing goods and services with the incentive of profit. His views on economic policy were shaped during his tenure as an economic consultant for the Boston Consulting Group. Reflecting on his experiences, he noted the limitations imposed by concentrations of power in other countries, and he pledged to address similar issues in Israel, aiming to create an environment that fosters healthy competition and growth.

In summary, Netanyahu's economic vision revolves around promoting a free-market system that incentivizes individual initiative, healthy competition, and economic growth while addressing concentrations of power that could impede progress.

Benjamin Netanyahu's stance on counter-terrorism has been deeply influenced by personal tragedy and extensive experience in both military operations and strategic thinking. His unequivocal condemnation of terrorism as "evil per se" reflects a commitment to democratic values and a belief in resolving conflicts through argument and debate.

Netanyahu's hardened position against terrorists is rooted in the tragic death of his brother, Yoni Netanyahu, during the hostage-rescue mission at Operation Entebbe. This personal loss has shaped his resolute stance against terrorism.

As an individual who actively participated in counter-terrorist operations during his military service, Netanyahu has delved into the subject extensively, authoring three books on fighting terrorism. He conceptualizes terrorism as a form of totalitarianism, emphasizing its insidious nature by targeting victims with no direct connection to the terrorists' grievances. According to Netanyahu, terrorists instill fear by intentionally choosing victims who are not involved in their perceived cause, making every member of society a potential target.

In addressing the delicate balance between civil liberties and security, Netanyahu acknowledges the intrusion that active anti-terror activities pose on individuals being monitored. He argues that during periods of sustained terrorist attacks, there should be a shift toward prioritizing security, but this should be regularly reviewed. Netanyahu emphasizes the importance of guarding civil liberties and individual privacy, suggesting that additional powers granted to security services require periodic renewal and judicial oversight.

Netanyahu advocates for tighter immigration laws as a preemptive measure against terrorism. He argues for stricter background checks on potential immigrants and the real possibility of deportation, emphasizing the need to bring an end to what he calls an "era of immigration free-for-all."

Crucially, Netanyahu warns against governments conflating terrorists with legitimate political groups that may hold various views. He urges the distinction between groups that participate in democracy, even if they hold extremist views, and those tiny fringes that use similar ideas as a pretext to step outside the democratic system.

Netanyahu's work on counter-terrorism, particularly his book "Terrorism: How the West Can Win," earned admiration from figures like Ronald Reagan. The former U.S. president recommended Netanyahu's book to senior officials in his administration, highlighting the international recognition of Netanyahu's insights into combating terrorism.

Death Penalty

In 2017, Benjamin Netanyahu, as Prime Minister of Israel, called for the imposition of the death penalty on the perpetrator of the 2017 Halamish stabbing attack. Representatives in his government subsequently introduced a bill to the Knesset that would allow the death penalty for terrorism. In a preliminary vote in January 2018, 52 members of the Israeli parliament voted in favor of making it easier for judges to hand down the death penalty, while 49 opposed it. However, the proposed amendment to the penal code would still require three more readings to become law. The move reflects Netanyahu's stance on taking a strong approach against terrorism.

LGBT Rights

Netanyahu has expressed support for equal rights for the LGBT community, stating that the struggle for every person to be recognized as equal before the law is ongoing. He acknowledged that there is still a long way to go but emphasized that Israel is among the most open countries globally regarding LGBT rights. During an event at the Knesset for the annual community rights day, Netanyahu reinforced the idea that every person is created in the image of God, signaling his commitment to inclusivity. However, it's worth noting that despite Netanyahu's support, some members of his coalition government's parties opposed same-sex marriage.

Ethiopian Jewish Integration

In 2015, following protests by the Ethiopian Jewish community against police brutality, Netanyahu pledged to bring a comprehensive plan to the government to assist the community in every way. He condemned racism and discrimination, vowing to transform them into contemptible and despicable actions within Israeli society. This commitment came in response to protests by Ethiopian Jews who faced challenges and discrimination, particularly in their interactions with law enforcement. Netanyahu's acknowledgment of the need for change reflects his stance on promoting inclusivity and addressing social injustices within Israeli society.

Benjamin Netanyahu is a proponent of the integration of the African Hebrew Israelites of Jerusalem into Israeli society. This community, which underwent an "exodus" from America to Israel in 1967, has found support from Netanyahu, who participates in celebrations commemorating their journey. In 2012, the Prime Minister expressed appreciation for the cooperative efforts aimed at including the Hebrew Israelite community within Israeli society. Netanyahu views the experiences of this community in the land of Israel as an integral part of the broader Israeli experience. This stance reflects a commitment to fostering inclusivity and recognizing diverse communities within the fabric of Israeli society.

Benjamin Netanyahu's views on Iran have been shaped by a deep-seated concern over the perceived threat posed by the Iranian government. In a notable 2007 interview, Netanyahu drew a stark comparison between Nazi Germany and the Islamic Republic of Iran, emphasizing the urgency of preventing Iran from acquiring nuclear weapons. This sentiment was reiterated in subsequent remarks, where he characterized Iran as the greatest threat Israel had ever faced.

Netanyahu's stance on Iran continued to evolve, and in a speech before the UN General Assembly in 2009, he emphasized the global ramifications of the Iranian regime's motivations, describing it as fueled by fanaticism and posing a threat not only to Israel but to civilization at large. This perspective led to a shift in focus, with some speculating that Netanyahu's foreign policy moved away from the Palestinian issue and towards countering the Iranian threat.

The Prime Minister has consistently advocated for a robust approach to address Iran's nuclear ambitions. He set a "red line" at 90% uranium enrichment, signaling that crossing this threshold would be intolerable for Israel. Netanyahu's use of a bomb graphic during a UN speech highlighted his concerns about Iran's progress in uranium enrichment, even though Mossad's assessment at the time suggested that Iran was not ready to enrich uranium to the levels required for a nuclear bomb.

Critics, including former Israeli officials, accused Netanyahu of exploiting the Iranian threat for political gain, arguing that he used it as a means to achieve various political objectives. Some contended that the Prime Minister's declarations unnecessarily heightened fear among the Israeli public, especially given Israel's limited involvement in the negotiations regarding Iran's nuclear program.

Despite international complexities, Netanyahu's position on Iran remained steadfast. The U.S. military's 2020 airstrike in Baghdad, targeting Iranian General Qasem Soleimani, received praise from Netanyahu, who commended the decisive action taken by then-U.S. President Donald Trump in response to the Iranian threat.

Benjamin Netanyahu became embroiled in a sensitive legal matter involving conflicting commitments made to the family of American terror victim Daniel Wultz and the Government of China. The case centered on allegations of terror financing against the Bank of China in a U.S. District Court. Netanyahu reportedly faced challenges in balancing commitments made to the Wultz family and diplomatic relations with China.

The Prime Minister was reported to have initially promised U.S. Representative Ileana Ros-Lehtinen full cooperation in the terror-financing case against the Bank of China. However, conflicting commitments were allegedly made to the Government of China prior to Netanyahu's state visit to China in May 2013. The delicate situation brought attention to the complexities of managing international relations and legal obligations.

Attorney David Boies, representing the Wultz family, emphasized the importance of allowing American courts to hear critical evidence in the case, despite diplomatic pressures. The issue gained prominence, with Ros-Lehtinen raising it during a congressional delegation to Israel in August 2013. She stressed the significance of Israel providing the necessary support for the Wultz family's lawsuit.

U.S. Representative Debbie Wasserman Schultz also expressed her involvement in seeking justice for the Wultz family and ensuring accountability for all parties involved, including the Bank of China. The case underscored the challenges faced by leaders like Netanyahu in navigating diplomatic relations while addressing legal matters with international implications.

During the 2023 Israel–Hamas war, Netanyahu advocated for Israel to assume "overall security responsibility" over the Gaza Strip. He expressed concerns about the eruption of Hamas terror and emphasized the importance of maintaining security in the region. This stance reflected Netanyahu's approach to defense and security matters, showcasing his commitment to safeguarding Israel against perceived threats.

Benjamin Netanyahu has consistently emphasized the importance of addressing and controlling illegal immigration, viewing it as a critical issue that impacts not only national security but also the social fabric and identity of the nation. In his 1995 book, "Fighting Terrorism: How Democracies Can Defeat Domestic and International Terrorism," Netanyahu argued strongly in favor of tightening immigration laws in the West as a crucial strategy in combating terrorism. He expressed the need to bring an end to the "era of immigration free-for-all."

In 2012, under Netanyahu's leadership, the Israeli government enacted the "Prevention of Infiltration Law," a policy that mandated the automatic detention of all individuals, including asylum-seekers, who entered Israel without permission. This move was met with criticism from organizations such as Amnesty International, which deemed it an affront to international law. The law aimed to address the increasing number of people, around 60,000, who had crossed into Israel from various African countries between 2009 and 2013. Netanyahu characterized this phenomenon as a serious threat to Israel's social fabric, national security, and identity. Many of these migrants were held in detention camps in the Negev desert.

When the Supreme Court of Israel declared the "Prevention of Infiltration Law" illegal due to concerns about immediate and indefinite detention of asylum seekers from Africa, Netanyahu responded by seeking new legislation to navigate around the Supreme Court ruling.

Netanyahu's stance on immigration extends beyond Israel's borders, as he has been critical of what he perceives as the overly open immigration policies of European Union (EU) nations. He has urged leaders of countries such as Hungary, Slovakia, Czech Republic, and Poland to close their borders to illegal immigration, aligning himself with a more restrictive approach to immigration issues. This reflects his broader perspective on the challenges and implications of immigration, both within Israel and in the international context.

Benjamin Netanyahu was born in Tel Aviv to parents Benzion Netanyahu (original name Mileikowsky) and Tzila (Cela; née Segal). His mother was born in 1912 in Petah Tikva, then part of Ottoman Palestine and now Israel. While all of his grandparents were born in the Russian Empire (present-day Belarus, Lithuania, and Poland), his mother's parents emigrated to Minneapolis in the United States.

Netanyahu is also connected to Rabbi Eliyahu of Vilna (the Vilna Gaon) on his paternal side. His father, Benzion Netanyahu, was a prominent figure—a professor of Jewish history at Cornell University, editor of the Encyclopaedia Hebraica, and a senior aide to Ze'ev Jabotinsky. Benzion Netanyahu remained active in research and writing well into his nineties. Notably, he expressed controversial views about the Palestinian people, suggesting severe measures in the event of a conflict.

Regarding the Palestinian people, Benzion Netanyahu once stated that they would not be able to endure a war with Israel, which he described as including actions such as withholding food, preventing education, and cutting off electrical power. He believed that such measures would lead them to leave the area, emphasizing the outcome's dependency on the war's course and Israel's success in battles.

Benjamin Netanyahu's paternal grandfather, Nathan Mileikowsky, was a prominent Zionist rabbi and fundraiser for the Jewish National Fund (JNF). Tragically, Netanyahu's older brother, Yonatan, lost his life during Operation Entebbe in Uganda in 1976. His younger brother, Iddo, pursued a career as a radiologist and writer. All three brothers served in the elite Sayeret Matkal reconnaissance unit of the Israel Defense Forces.

Benjamin Netanyahu has been married three times. His first marriage was to Miriam Weizmann, whom he met in Israel. They married in 1972 after both studying in the United States. The couple had one daughter, Noa, born on April 29, 1978. However, the marriage ended in divorce in 1978 after Netanyahu had an affair with Fleur Cates, a non-Jewish British student he met at MIT.

In 1981, Netanyahu married Fleur Cates, who converted to Judaism. After moving to Israel, their marriage faced challenges, and Cates sued for divorce in 1988.

Netanyahu's third and current wife is Sara Ben-Artzi. They met when she was working as a flight attendant on an El Al flight from New York to Israel. They got married in 1991 and have two sons: Yair, born on July 26, 1991, and Avner, born on October 10, 1994. Yair served as a soldier in the IDF Spokesperson's Unit, while Avner is a national Bible champion and former soldier in the IDF Combat Intelligence Collection Corps.

In 1993, Netanyahu admitted to having had an affair with Ruth Bar, his public relations adviser, and made a public confession on live television. Despite the challenges, he and Sara repaired their marriage, and Netanyahu went on to be elected as the leader of Likud.

Over the years, Netanyahu's private life has occasionally been subject to media scrutiny, with reports of friendships and alleged affairs. In 1996, it was reported that he had a 20-year friendship with Katherine Price-Mondadori, an Italian-American woman. Netanyahu criticized such intrusions into his private life, attributing them to political rivals.

As of October 2009, Netanyahu is a grandfather, as his daughter Noa Netanyahu-Roth, married to Daniel Roth, gave birth to a boy named Shmuel. In 2011, Noa and her husband had a second son named David, and in 2016, they had a daughter. Noa is a baalat teshuva, indicating someone born to a secular family who returned to Orthodox Judaism, and she lives in Mea Shearim with her family.

Benjamin Netanyahu has been dealing with health issues, specifically Right Bundle Branch Block (RBBB), since around 2003. To address this condition, on July 22, 2023, he underwent a medical procedure in which a pacemaker was implanted in his body. The pacemaker is a medical device designed to regulate his heart rhythm and manage the effects of the RBBB. This development has played a role in shaping his overall health and well-being in recent years.

Authored Books:

Benjamin Netanyahu has authored several books throughout his career, covering topics ranging from terrorism to international relations. Here is a list of his published works:

"International Terrorism: Challenge and Response" (1981) - Published by Transaction Publishers. ISBN: 978-0-87855-894-0.

"Terrorism: How the West Can Win" (1987) - Published by Avon. ISBN: 978-0-380-70321-0.

"Fighting Terrorism: How Democracies Can Defeat Domestic and International Terrorism" (1995) - Published by Farrar, Straus and Giroux. ISBN: 978-0-374-15492-9.

"A Durable Peace: Israel and Its Place Among the Nations" (1999, originally published in 1993) - Published by Grand Central Publishing. ISBN: 978-0-446-52306-6.

"Bibi: My Story" (2022) - Published by Simon and Schuster. ISBN: 978-1-6680-0844-7.

Made in United States
Troutdale, OR
10/09/2024

23607374R00030